Adventure Abounds

A Beginner and Kid Friendly
Guide to Getting Outside in the
Snoqualmie Area of Washington

Tiffany Green, DC

Adventure Abounds: A Beginner and Kid Friendly Guide to Getting Outside in the Snoqualmie Area of Washington

Adventure Abounds was written by Dr. Tiffany Green of Snoqualmie Optimal Health Chiropractic as a guide to encourage patients to jump into active healthy lifestyle choices, in an easy and inviting way. Whether you are using this book to discover the outdoors on your own, or using this book as a family, Adventure Abounds aims to make getting outside more accessible and fun!

Enjoy the book and by all means please share it with others! You know, in the non-plagiarism way! 😊

Thank you for reading!

Dr. Tiffany

Front Book Cover Photo at Gold Creek Pond:

Taken by Jubilant Studios

Adventure Abounds: A Beginner and Kid Friendly Guide to Getting Outside in the Snoqualmie Area of Washington

Library of Congress Control Number: 2019902781

ISBN: 9781791384456

Published by Kindle Direct Publishing

Disclaimer: There are inherent dangers when exploring the great outdoors. Every effort is made to help you prepare and stay safe. Ultimately, your safety is your responsibility.

Let the
Adventures
Begin!

Why I Wrote This Book

My "it" place, the place where I go to get away from it all. The place where I feel calm and ready to take on the world. Stepping out into nature has always been grounding for my anxious and fast paced personality, even as a kid. As an adult, I have come to recognize the calming effect that the Outdoors has on me. My tendency like many is to get pulled into the fast-paced motion of society. It's easy to become exhausted just trying to keep up, let alone trying to "succeed" in life. Getting *Outside* calms me, revitalizes me and makes me smile. It connects me with myself, my higher power and my family and friends. It is there for me when I'm not sure how to be there for myself. It ALWAYS brings me back to who I am and what I should be doing.

In my career life, I am a Chiropractor. It might seem funny to you that a Chiropractor is writing this book. It might help you to know that there are different kinds of Chiropractors. Some are more symptom based, some are more wellness based and others are in the middle. I am a wellness based Chiropractor. Active living and getting outside come up OFTEN in our practice. I noticed a reoccurring theme in my patients' questions. How do I get started? Where do I go? I'm so out of shape! How do I know I'm not going to be in agony after adventuring out!? They had no idea where to start.

Those of us who LOVE and LIVE the outdoors probably take its accessibility for granted. For those individuals who have never been on a hike, haven't ridden a bike in years, who have never set foot in a state park or who haven't the slightest idea where to camp, *Getting Outdoors* seems like a huge hassle if not impossible!

On a personal level I know the huge mental health benefit getting outside can have. As a Chiropractor, I know the huge physical health benefits the outdoors can have. Not everyone is going to start with an activity that would qualify as exercise, but let's say an individual starts with visiting one of our State Parks. Imagine them walking along the slow-moving river, their kids playing on the playground and one of the kids saying, "Hey dad, let's go check out this trail!" This is where it starts! Nature pulls us in with curiosity and intrigue. We have an inborn desire to explore when opportunity presents itself. Sometimes putting ourselves in front of opportunity is just what we need to take the small steps that lead to leaps in our physical and mental health.

The idea for this book was created with my patients and the love I have for exploring the Outdoors in mind. Sharing opportunities to explore our amazing surroundings brings me joy. This book is meant to give beginners, young families and individuals that just want to get back to it, the opportunity to do just that! I'm grateful for my family who went "exploring" and "adventuring" with me to over 30 different locations. Looking to the future, I hope to add to this book.

My goal is to keep it simple and fun, and get you and your family outside! The book is organized from easy to most difficult. Enjoy!

Enjoy!

Dr. Tiffany Green

Snoqualmie Optimal Health Chiropractic

Getting Started

Some of you might know what to bring, while others might not, so let's go over some essentials! This list is not all-inclusive, but it is a great place to start! I've broken it down into types of adventuring. For most adventures, you will need a Discover Pass or Northwest Forest Pass. As of 2019, both passes are $30 for an annual pass. Discover Day Passes are $10 and Northwest Forest Day Passes are $5. Discover passes can be purchased at our more popular state parks, online and in some recreational stores. Northwest Forest Passes are available at the North Bend Ranger Station, online and in some recreational stores.

Hitting up a Local/State Park

- Athletic shoes and comfortable clothing
- Layers—It can often be colder at elevation, and or near water. During the fall, patchy fog can create cold pockets as well.
- Snacks
- Water
- Sunscreen
- Tip: Extra clothes and a towel in the car if you're near water and have young children on your outing 😊

Hiking

- Athletic shoes
- Comfortable clothing with layers

- Rain slick, if appropriate
- A backpack (at least one for the group)
- Baby/Toddler carrying backpack specifically made for hiking if you have a small one that needs carried
- A small first aid kit (keep in the backpack)
- Fully charged phone with GPS capabilities
- Water
- Snacks
- Sunscreen
- Tip: For hikes with a lot of water and young children in tow, extra socks or waterproof shoes might be helpful ☺

Biking

- Athletic shoes and comfortable clothing
- One extra layer, if appropriate
- Rain slick, if appropriate
- Water reservoir backpack with a bungee carrying system on the outside and/or additional pockets to hold snacks and one layer
- Tire repair kit
- Small hand-held pump
- Helmet
- Hand protection, if wanted (Bike Gloves)
- Sunscreen
- A small first aid kit

Swimming

- Sunscreen
- Towels

- Warm clothes to put on after if not a super-hot day
- Water shoes
- Water floaties because they're fun!
- Life vests, if needed
- Swimsuits
- Goggles, snorkel, etc
- Snacks

Camping

- Tent
- Sleeping bags rated down to at least 32 degrees
- Pillows if you want them
- Padding for under the sleeping bags
  - Cots
  - Air mattresses
  - Sleeping pads
  - TIP: With smaller kids you can get a family of four on a king sized air mattress if you turn it sideways ☺
- Extra clothes—it can be REALLY cold late in the evening/night and in the early morning (hence the 32 degree sleeping bag)
- Lots of wood if fires are allowed (ask the local ranger station and or camp hosts)
  - TIP: If fires are banned you can use a small propane fire pit. They'll keep you warm at night and you can roast marshmallows on them ☺
- Foldable chairs for sitting around the campsite/fire
- A nice cooler to bring your food
- Portable stove top with propane

- Pots and pans
- Scrubber and soap
- Utensils, plates, cups, etc.
- Baby wipes for cleaning
- Paper towels
- Garbage bags
- Foil
- First aid kit
- TIP: Unless you want animals in your tent and at your campsite, lock all "smelly" things—food, garbage, toiletries, etc.—In bear proof containers or in the car overnight

That first time doing any of these activities can be a little nerve racking not knowing what to bring or if everyone will like it! There is a reason they call it the Great Outdoors ☺ Odds are, you and your family will have a great time! So, take that leap of faith and jump in!

Safety First and General Rules

It is true that there are some inherent dangers in the outdoors. That said, there are a few tips that significantly lesson your odds of getting in trouble. Here's a safety checklist for you.

- Tell someone where you are going and how long you plan on being there (IE, for the day or overnight)
- Take a fully charged cellphone with you. If you have it, also bring a portable charger.
- Download a GPS app (like All Trails) before you go. Check in with it frequently to track your progress.
- Bring an outdoor specific first aid kit (you can find them on Amazon)
- Do not veer off the trail
- If you find yourself lost, stop and look at your GPS, stay on marked trails and don't hesitate to ask a fellow hiker
  - Getting lost on Marked Trails can happen, especially on Tiger and Cougar Mountain where a series of trails link up
- Have bear spray accessible from a waist belt or backpack side pocket (reachable without taking anything off)
  - Can be used on Bears and Cougars, or even self-defense
- Always have snacks and water
- Do not eat berries UNLESS you KNOW what you are eating. We are so lucky to have TONS of edible berries in our forests, but you need to

know what is what. The same goes for mushrooms! You can become very sick, very quickly.

- Always bring at least one extra layer
- Look before you leap in regards to bodies of water
- Do not swim in currents and wear a life vest if you are in the water
- Always stay with children—in the water and on the trail/at the park
- Always wear helmets if biking
- Do not try to pet, lure or engage wildlife…even if it's "just a deer"
- When camping, do not leave food out overnight—it will be animal bait…including bear. Also, do not leave food, nice smelling items (some even say personal care items) in your tent for the same reason.

There are some general rules to abide by when you're enjoying the outdoors. These preserve our lands and help others enjoy their experience too!

Most trails and parks are open dawn to dusk. We've got friends that have accidentally been locked in a parking lot, so if you think you're going to be cutting it close bring flashlights and park OUTSIDE of the gates.

If you see anything of concern, report it. This can be a suspicious person, an animal that is acting strange or a trail or park danger.

Most if not all, of the adventures in this book are "no motorized vehicles." So remember to check signs on entry.

Trails all have leash laws. Please abide by them. It may be true that your dog is non-aggressive and responds to your call, but your animal may encounter an animal or dog who is not dog friendly. The rule is there to protect everyone.

Pack in and pack out. Whatever you bring in needs to be brought out or disposed of in a proper receptacle. This includes garbage and your animal's droppings. Do not leave your animals poop bag on the side of the trail. You are responsible for taking it out of the park or down the trail. If you need to use the restroom where there is no restroom available there are two accepted philosophies. Both involve you leaving the trail and getting out of sight.

One option is to bury any toilet paper or stools that you leave. The second is to pack it out in a zip lock bag. The choice is yours, but please don't leave your bathroom habits visible.

On large trails, the rule of thumb is to stay to the right. When you see oncoming trail users move to the right so they can pass safely.

Do not feed the wildlife. This creates dependent animals that are not afraid of humans.

Best Of

Best Rainy-Day Adventures

- Swamp Trail to Big Tree Trail and Back
- Twin Falls Ollalie State Park
- Cougar Mountain

Best Kid Adventures

- The North Bend BMX Bike Park
- Twin Falls Ollalie State Park
- Rattlesnake Lake

Best First Hikes for Adults

- Twin Falls to the Lookout Bench
- Denny Creek
- Asahel Curtis Nature Trail

Best First Hikes for Kids

- Twin Falls to the Lookout Bench
- Swamp Monster Trail and back
- Tanner Landing Park Trail along the river and back

Best Picnic Spots

- Snoqualmie Point Park
- Gold Creek Pond

- Nolte State Park

Best First Time Camping

- Lake Easton State Park
- Kanaskat Palmer State Park
- Tinkham Campground

Best Campsites with Walk-In Availability

- Lake Kachess
- Tinkham Campground

Best Family Friendly Mountain Bike/BMX Trails

- Duthie Hill
- North Bend BMX Bike Park

Best Long-Distance Low Grade/Pitch Trails

- Snoqualmie Valley Trail
- Iron Horse Trail

Best Swimming Spots

- Lake Wilderness (summer lifeguard)
- Lake Sammamish (summer lifeguard)
- Rattlesnake Lake

Best Accessibility

- Rattlesnake Lake—parking and easy access to a paved trail and lake picnic areas
- Snoqualmie Point Park—parking and easy access to amazing views and picnic benches
- Top of Snoqualmie Falls—pay to park, easy access to viewing decks

Best State Park Playgrounds

- Lake Sammamish State Park
- Nolte State Park
- Lake Easton State Park

Best places to go for Versatility

- Torgusen Park—rock climbing, biking, walking path, playground, skate park, picnic, fields
- Lake Sammamish State Park—swimming, boat rentals, playground, picnic, fields, biking, walking trails, fishing, boat launch
- Lake Wilderness—boat rentals, biking, walking trails, swimming, disc golf, picnic

Three Forks Natural Area

Season: Year-Round **Difficulty:** 1/4

Parking: Crowded **Time:** 1-4hrs

Getting There: Can be accessed from downtown Snoqualmie or downtown North Bend. Be sure to enter Three Forks Natural Area in your GPS/phone and follow.

The Adventure: A short walk through the woods will take you to the shores of the Middle and North Forks of the Snoqualmie. We ventured out to this spot at the beginning of summer when the waters were still a bit high. Over the summer we frequently drove by the area. We would see cars on either side of the street and the parking lot full. As

15

the waters recede no doubt this makes a great wading, rock-skipping and all day hang out!

Our Favorite Part: The gorgeous view of the Valley and the Snoqualmie River.

Weeks Falls: Ollalie State Park

East of North Bend: Hiking, Water, Picnic, Field Play

Season: Year-Round   **Difficulty:** 1/4

Parking: Plentiful   **Time:** 1-2 hours

Getting There: Ollalie State Park is a large and long state park spanning the area between exits 34 and 38 on I-90.

Weeks Falls is off of exit 38. Take a right-hand turn onto Homested Valley Road which becomes Frontage Road. Look for the State Park sign. Turn left into the park.

The Adventure: We loved this adventure! We've always been such fans of the exit 34 portion of Ollalie State Park that we hadn't ventured to Weeks Falls. Perfect for littles, the approximately 1.5 mile roundtrip adventure takes you along the river with rushing water, broad canopy and HUGE old growth trees! At the end of the Weeks Falls Trail you will come into a small handicap accessible parking lot with a short-paved path to an overlook of Weeks Falls and a small hydro-electric plant! How cool for kids! Our kids loved learning about the hydro-electric plant (ok sort of—they were more interested in the falls and HUGE trees), but they were interested. ☺ Great place for an accessible view point, younger kids and adults who just want to get back into shape!

Our Favorite Part: The falls, The river and the HUGE trees! As you can see we were able to fit both children in one of them!

Snoqualmie Point Park

Season: Year-Round   **Difficulty:** 1/4

Parking: Fair   **Time:** 1 hour

Getting There: I-90 Eastbound to Exit 27. Turn right and follow the road around a bend to the left. You will see LOTS of parked cars. Do not park (they are mountain biking). Follow the road to the end to the official Snoqualmie Point Park parking lot.

The Adventure: This is probably one of my favorite locally accessible spots. It is an absolutely breathtaking picnic spot. We have family that would love to spend time with us outside, but have difficulty navigating challenging terrain. The easy parking, paved pathway, breathtaking views and spots to sit make this an ideal place to take individuals who want to get outside, but accessibility makes it difficult. It's beauty and peacefulness have appeared in several family photos and are likely to catch your attention! Enjoy this close gem!

Our Favorite Part: The views and the wild flowers! Great place for a picnic!

Alpental Exploration

At Snoqualmie Summit: Water, hiking, photography, exploring, snow fields

Season: May-June   **Difficulty:** 1/4

Parking: Plentiful   **Time:** 1-2 hours

Getting There: Take I-90 East Bound to exit 52. Turn left off the exit. The road will fork in two directions shortly after the freeway. In the winter, with large snow pack the route to the left will be blocked and you are naturally routed to the right toward Alpental Ski Area. If the snowpack is low, you *will* be able to go to the left under the freeway. DO NOT go under the freeway, this will take you the wrong direction. You want to stay to the right. Remember this fork will NOT be visible if the snow pack is still blocking it. If this is the case, it will seem that there is only one direction to the road. You should be good. That said you can always enter Alpental into your GPS ☺.

Drive the approximate 3 minutes to Alpental's parking lot. After the ski season this parking lot is monitored by the National Forest Service. You will need a $5 day pass (online or at the ranger station at the summit) or an Annual National Forest Pass.

The Adventure: This is one of our family's favorite unknown adventures! It's short lived and the window depends on the snow pack, but it's typically May-June. Once the ski resort closes, this area becomes absolutely magical with massive snow melt and fun snow fields. You can explore the lower snow fields with sleds, walk along the service road and see how many waterfalls you can count, peer over the fun bridge at the rushing water below. It is truly neat, and is an opportunity for kids to learn about snow melt and the states of water.

Safety Note: The rushing streams **CUT** through the snow. **DO NOT WALK ON THE SNOW NEXT TO THE RUSHING WATERS.** This is not safe because it may not be stable under your feet and as you'll see, the waters can be extremely fast and wide enough to really get an individual in trouble. So enjoy from afar. 😊

21

Our favorite part: Catching it just right where we get to see waterfalls, rushing rivers **AND** play in the snow!

Iron Horse Trail/John Wayne Trail/Palouse to Cascades State Park Trail

North Bend: Hiking, Biking, Nature Walks, Berry Picking

Season: Year-Round

Parking: Plentiful

Difficulty: 1/4

Time: 1+ hrs

Getting There: Take Exit 32 in North Bend and turn South (right turn if coming from Snoqualmie). Head up the hill to Rattlesnake Lake. Follow the road to the left rather than turning into Rattlesnake Lake. Immediately there will be a left-hand turn into the Iron Horse State Park parking lot. Since it's a state park you will need a $10 day pass or $30 annual pass. You can park at the lake for free, but parking can get VERY difficult on warm days.

The Adventure: It's yours for the making! We've used this trail many times; for a walk, for a bike ride, and as an access point for Cedar Butte. You can even take it all the way to Vantage and then from the town of Lind to the Idaho-Washington border town of Tekoa! We have yet to do that, but it is a pleasant fun multi-use trail! This year we dropped my husband and his bike at Hyak (at the pass) and he rode the twenty something miles down to North Bend, including a 2-mile Tunnel!!! So, the possibilities are endless! During early summer berries are plentiful, so if you've got berry picking kids like ours, don't expect to go fast! 😊 Apparently, they need to recharge on berries every two minutes!

Our Favorite Part: The possibilities and the berries!

Rattlesnake Lake

North Bend: Nature Walks, Swimming, Biking, Educational Center, Fishing, Boat Launch, Tours

Season: Year-Round   **Difficulty:** 1/4

Parking: Variable   **Time:** 1-3 hrs

Getting There: Take Exit 32 off of I-90 and head South. Head up Cedar Falls Road. The road ends at the Lake. Parking is free as long as you are not in the small state park parking lot on the left (Iron Horse).

The Adventure: There are so many adventures to be had at Rattlesnake Lake; from the Cedar River Watershed on a rainy day, to swimming on a hot summer day! The Cedar

River Watershed is a free walk-through education center. It even has a rain drum garden! Paid tours of our Watershed are available during the Summer months. We have yet to do one, but we hear they are amazing. You get to access areas that are not accessible to the general public such as the historic town of Cedar Falls, Masonry Dam, Chester Morse Lake and Cedar Falls Waterfall! They're super affordable, so I honestly can't say why we haven't done it yet! Soon!

There is a nice paved trail along the southeast shore of Rattlesnake Lake that most don't know about. Walkable, bikeable and accessible, it's gorgeous and quiet. From the parking walk toward the lake. You will cross the lower road that accesses the accessible parking. To the left of the boat launch you will see the paved trail. Continue to your left. The trail follows the shore. Trails to the right from the parking lot will go to the other side of the lake to the popular Rattlesnake Ledge Trail. This trail is a beautiful hike but is more advanced than this book.

Note: The accessible parking is just before the boat launch and right at the beach. If you will be accessing the paved trail and need accessible parking this should be a nice place for you to park and for everyone to enjoy the trail and the beach. If going to the beach, there is a short walk required after the paved trail to the beach. There are multiple places to place your chairs, blankets, etc that are firm grassy plots of land. These places are easier to bring walkers, wheelchairs and other mobility devices as compared to the sandy shores directly next to the water.

As previously mentioned, adjacent to the paved trail and the accessible parking is the main swimming beach and boat launch. We've used this beach many times whether it's jumping in (brrr) with swimsuits and life vests or going out in the kayak! Popular with the stand-up paddle board community this lake is great for summer recreating and barbequing!

Follow any of the trails to secluded areas and with a fishing license you can drop a line. If you have a fishing boat, you can drop in at the boat launch verses the shore.

You can see why parking can become a HUGE problem in the warm summer months! This place really does have something for everyone!

Our Favorite Part: The versatility!

Gold Creek Pond

Snoqualmie Pass: Snowshoeing, Nature Walks, Water, Photography

Season: Year-Round

Parking: Variable

Difficulty: 1/4

Time: 1-2 hrs

Getting There: Take I-90 East to exit 54. Turn left off the freeway. Go past the I-90 Westbound entrance. Turn right on NFSR 4832 slightly after I-90. Follow the road for approximately 1 mile and then turn left onto NFSR 142 into the park. There is quite a bit of parking, but it's also VERY popular on nice weekend days. You will need a NWF pass.

In the Winter: NFSR 142 will not be plowed. Park along NFSR 4832. You will need a SNO-PARK PASS. You get this from the National forest service, but it is different than a day or annual pass. Park and snowshoe in.

The Adventure: Our Gold Creek Pond experience feels more like a get-away than an adventure. It's beautiful and one of the most serene places in our area. On a calm sunny day, you can see perfect mountain reflections off the water. There is a beautiful paved 1.1 mile trail around the "Pond" that feels more like a lake. Coming from the parking lot there is one trail that splits into two. Going left will quickly take you to a beautiful picnic area where you can relax, snap photos and grab a bite to eat. Going right will take you all the way around the 1.1 mile trail and back to the picnic area. In the Fall, you can find hundreds of small salmon spawning in the creeks leading into Gold Creek Pond! So cool for us and the kids! In the Winter, you can snowshoe around that same trail! Remember, you will need a Sno-Park pass to park on NFSR 4832!

Our Favorite Part: The beauty of the spot. After seeing Gold Creek Pond, we made it our last family photo shoot location. You just can't beat it!

Tanner Landing Park

North Bend: Hiking, Nature Walks, Water, Photography, Fishing

Season: Year-Round   **Difficulty:** 1/4

Parking: Plentiful   **Time:** .5-1 hr

Getting There: From North Bend Way, just outside of downtown North Bend, turn onto Mt. Si Road. Quickly, after you turn onto Mt. Si Road, just before the bridge, turn into Tanner Landing Park. The sign is at the entrance, but the road looks like a general access road. Turn onto it, it will turn left and end at a parking lot. Do not use your GPS to get to this location. As of the time of this print, GPS does not pull up a specific location. You may input Little Si Trailhead to get you going in the right direction. Once you are on Mt. Si Road follow the above directions.

The Adventure: This is one of our family's favorite spots! It's never crowded. It's gorgeous, and easily done with children! There's a picnic bench at the entrance, but we usually prefer to find some rocks along the river and enjoy a picnic lunch or dinner on the water. There are two trails that leave the parking lot. One goes into the field and is quickly lost by overgrown grass. The other goes into the trees and along the river. This is the trail that we usually take. You can take this trail approximately a mile to the Snoqualmie Valley Trail. From there, you can go further on the Snoqualmie Valley Trail, but we usually turn around. It's a very easy trail and the scenery can't be beat! It would be a perfect spot to test out your hiking legs if you've never hiked or if you're introducing kids to hiking.

Often, we forget that walking on uneven ground is harder than a flat paved surface. Your body works harder to do this. That is why we recommend that your first time out be on a flat but uneven trail. You can test out your distance and mobility over uneven terrain without the hill! 😊 This trail and the bottom portion of Twin Falls are great training grounds!

Our Favorite Part: The ability to have a quick outdoor adventure here! Often, we will stop for a quick picnic and walk along the river.

Lake Wilderness Park

Maple Valley: Hiking, Nature Walks, Swimming, Biking, Disc Golf, Playground, Tennis Courts, Softball Field, Boat Launch (non-combustible engines), Boat Rentals and Fishing

Season: Year-Round   **Difficulty:** 1/4

Parking: Crowded   **Time:** 1-4 hrs

Getting There: Enter this into your GPS for the best directions. You will drive Highway 18 westbound to Maple Valley. Take the SE 231st Street exit. Turn left off of the exit onto a short section of 231st. Turn right at the light onto Maple Valley Highway. Shortly thereafter you will take another right-hand turn onto Witte Rd SE. Continue until 248th St. Turn left at 248th. There will be signs. Turn left into the parking lot.

The Adventure: When we lived in Renton, we frequented this park A LOT. Its shallow waters on top of a sandy beach made this a great place to take the kids swimming. Add to that bathrooms with showers and changing areas, lifeguards, a roped off safe swimming area, concessions and boat rentals; what more could you ask for?

When we weren't swimming, we enjoyed biking or walking the nearby Green to Cedar River Trail, which we knew as Lake Wilderness Trail. It has since become part of a project that is ongoing as of 2019 to connect the Cedar River Trail in Maple Valley to the Green River Trail in Flaming Geyser State Park south of Black Diamond.

After moving to North Bend, my son and I took a trip to the park when our car was in a nearby shop. We walked from Witte and Maple Valley Highway—that may have been a bit much for my four-year old! We were excited to check out the newly opened Gaffney's Grove 18 Hole Disc Golf Course. We met two older gentlemen that were in their 70s that reminded me of a real-life John and Max from *Grumpy Old Men,* but in their happy getting along state! They were really nice, letting Zander watch them for a couple of holes and even giving him a disc! What a fun experience! The Disc Golf Course has its own parking lot at 22500 SE 248th St, Maple Valley Wa.

Our Favorite Part: Surprisingly, we haven't been to the disc golf course as a family yet! Once we go as a family, I'm positive that the disc golf course and the swimming will be our favorites!

Nolte State Park

Southeast of Black Diamond: Swimming, Nature Walk, Biking, Fishing, Playground, Picnics, Horseshoes, Non-Motorized Boating

Season: Year-Round   **Difficulty:** 1/4

Parking: Variable   **Time:** 1-4 hr

Getting There: Put it into your GPS. Kanaskat-Palmer State park is just 4 miles away from Nolte State Park so consider doing both on the same day! State park means Discover Pass so don't forget yours! $10 for the day or $30 for the year.

The Adventure: This park was beautiful! It was one of the parks we briefly explored, so I can't wait to make it back! We were able to park easily, but I can imagine a busy parking lot on hot days. Stepping onto the grounds from the parking lot, the first thing my kids saw was the huge grassy field with a beautiful playground! The first thing that caught my eyes was the beautiful lake with its sandy swimming shore and fishing dock off to the side.

With its beauty, shade in places, swimming shore, dock, picnic shelters and a 1.4 mile trail around the lake the thought that jumped out in my mind was "This would be a great place to hang out with family or friends over a BBQ." That it would, and we plan on going back!

Our Favorite Part: The dock. 😊 The kids loved hanging out on it and can't wait to bring their fishing rods back!

Lake Kachess National Area

East of Snoqualmie Pass: Hiking, Swimming, Boating, Fishing, Camping, Picnics, Berries

Season: June-September   **Difficulty:** 1/4

Parking: Variable   **Time:** Hrs to Days

Getting There: Take I-90 East bound to the Lake Kachess exit. Turn left off the freeway and follow the signs and Kachess Lake Road for 5.5 miles. The road will come to a

T, go right into the park. This is on National Park lands and requires a pass to park. $5 for a day or $30 for the year.

The Adventure: Hands down our favorite new spot for the Summer of 2018! I spent a lot of time in Lake Tahoe as a young adult. Lake Kachess reminds me of a less busy, less touristy Lake Tahoe. Its crystal blue waters surrounded by trees and mountains take me back!

There are two day use areas at the park. Both offer swimming, sandy shores and crisp refreshing (ie cold) waters. Picnic benches and BBQ's can be found at each day use area. There are also two boat launches. At the south end you will find a motorized boat launch. At the north end you will find the non-motorized boat launch.

Around the campground, you will find the Little Kachess Trail and the Lakeshore Trail. All visitors are required to stop in at the gatehouse during business hours. Being new to the park, I rather enjoyed the informative stop. 😊 Map in hand, I was ready to explore!

Our first time here, the kids and I hit up both day use areas and thoroughly scoped out the walk-in campsites. The area has 26 trailer sites (with 23 of them being drive through) and 133 combination trailer/tent sites. Thirty-five of these sites are walk-in. Our family doesn't like to camp in rain or extreme heat, so walk-ins are just the ticket for us!

Kachess is broken into "Loops". The loop with the best walk-in availability and best layout (in our opinion) is Lodgecreek Loop. Lodgecreek Loop and Thetis Loop have the best walk-in availability for small groups. There are three main differences between Thetis Creek Loop and Lodgecreek Loop. Thetis Creek has a busier feel to it, and is more exposed, but is also close to the water. On a cooler day this greater sun exposure is probably preferred; not so much on a hot day. Although the water is nearby so at least you can keep jumping in to stay cool!

Labor Day of 2018 we headed back to Lake Kachess with friends. We were able to secure two sites right next to each other in Lodgecreek Loop. The kids loved riding their bikes around the loop and playing on the trails that went from the campgrounds to a central bathroom. Speaking of bathrooms, this one had running water! Not all of them do, so if you're looking for running water it might be worthwhile to call during business hours and ask which loops have restrooms with running water. 😊

If booking ahead, Box Canyon Loop was away from it all and had amazing sites nearly on the water. During our Labor Day stay, we walked over to Box Canyon via the Lakeshore Trail. We were shocked how COLD it was on the water. The wind was whipping across those refreshing waters and mother nature had the AC on full blast. That said, we will probably eventually book Box Canyon. It's just so beautiful! Bring hats and layers and you should be good to camp there too!

Side-note: We did try our hand at fishing and caught nothing. Although we did get to see bats coming out over the water as night fell. Individuals we talked to had much better luck out on the water verses the shore.

Our Favorite Part: The beauty of it all.

Keechelus Lake

East of the Summit: Exploring, Photography

Season: May-Oct

Difficulty: 1/4

Parking: Plentiful

Time: .5-1 hr

Getting There: Take exit 54 off of I-90. Take a right and take your first left before going into the ski resort. You will see a sign to Iron Horse, Hyak and Keechulus Trail. Follow this road past the Iron Horse State Park parking lot (on the right). The road will edge along Keechelus Lake. You will see two "official" and likely dry boat launches. Past these, you will see a gravel road that dead ends at the water. Drive as far as you can, park and explore!

The Adventure: Keechelus is a reservoir, and in being so offers many wonders to the young and old eye. Its waters rise and recede with the seasons. The receding waters make for cool little streams flowing toward the lake. Our kids love the scenery of it! Pure and simple, and picture worthy. Keechelus is apparently also known for its Kokanee fish. Stocked every year, we are excited to hit it up with our fishing poles and see what we can find!

Our Favorite Part: It's nice to have quick stops in your back pocket. This is one of those. It doesn't require a lot of time and it will please the kids!

Flaming Geyser State Park

South of Black Diamond: Hiking, Equestrian Use, Berries, Swimming/Wading, Picnics, Model Air Craft Flying, Interpretive Walk, Playground

Season: Year-Round   **Difficulty:** 1/4

Parking: Plentiful   **Time:** 1-4 hrs

Getting There: GPS works for this one.

The Adventure: This is another one that I wish we would have had more time to explore. As for the flaming geyser, if you go to see that you're going to be disappointed. If you go for the vast fields, the many picnic shelters, the river, fire pits, berry picking, hiking and or flying model aircraft; you'll have a blast! Flaming Geyser is a huge park that is great for entertaining and having a pleasant and relaxing day.

This park offers an ADA accessible interpretive trail and restrooms. The park is very long and laid out. If you are looking for ADA accessibility, I would check out the park yourself first and check out the State's ADA map at https://parks.state.wa.us/156/ADA-Recreation.

Probably what stood out the most about this park was its ability to host large groups: family reunions, birthday parties, and or work picnics. Their shelters are reservable and will hold 50 people. Definitely a great group option!

Our Favorite Part: The fact that they had a model airplane flying launch pad, complete with a flying field and several launch sites. How neat!

Lake Sammamish State Park

Issaquah: Hiking, Biking, Team Sports, Swimming, Boat Rentals, Paddle Board Rentals, Volleyball, Boat Launch, Playground

Season: Year-Round   **Difficulty:** 1/4

Parking: Plentiful   **Time:** 1-4 hrs

Getting There: Input into GPS.

The Adventure: We checked out this park on a warm Monday late morning. Surprisingly, it was not overcrowded! There are two swimming areas. Tibetts beach has rentals and concessions. Our group checked out Sunset Beach. The waters were warm as promised, and the kids had a great time!

There is a fantastic all accessible playground at Sunset Beach, as well as two other playground areas at the park.

Although we didn't get to check it out, Lake Sammamish has trails connecting the Sammamish Cove area to the Jensen Cove area. This is a beautiful park with lots to do and see. Be sure to check it out on a weekday, as it is known for crowds on the weekend!

Our Favorite Part: The warm waters! The kids basically jumped right in! The other mom and I did too!

Lake Easton State Park

Easton: Hiking, Biking, Swimming, Basketball, Boat Launch, Playground, Winter Activities, Amphitheater, Horse Shoe Pits, Fishing, Camping, Access to the Iron Horse Trail

Season: Year-Round

Parking: Fair

Difficulty: 1/4

Time: Hrs to Days

Getting There: Input into GPS. This is a State Park so you will need your Discover Pass.

The Adventure: This will likely become next year's favorite stormy Spring get away! Often when it's a rainy and dreary Spring in the Valley, it's overcast and dry in Easton. At a mere 40 min drive, it is well worth putting the

kids in the car and heading across the pass for a little vitamin D! The playground is ample and is situated perfectly across from the water. Our kids ran back and forth between the two. Our only challenge was keeping them out of the water despite cool temps!

We saw people with bikes no doubt looking to adventure on the miles of trails in the areas. With easy access to the Iron Horse Trail your adventures are limitless. Not much of a biker? Hike around on the trails bordering the lake, head up to the Iron Horse Trail or go out on the water. Fishing is also an option if you are more of the lounging type. ☺

Next year we hope to stay at the campground at Easton. Overall, I was very impressed. This would be a great place to go with a group of family or friends. The flush toilets, basketball court and playground all make this very family friendly. There is even a shower down by the lake, if you don't mind the short drive from the campsite.

There are two "campgrounds" in one at Lake Easton State Park. The first one is above the playground and beach, looking out over the water. This campground is specifically designed for RV's and even has a paved accessible site! The second campground is on the opposite end of the park near the Iron Horse Trail access point. This one consists of two loops. The loop nearest to the freeway was our least

favorite due to the road noise and occasional semi-truck viewing on I-90. I would go for that inside loop. ☺

Our Favorite Part: That it's an easy and fun get away in the Spring! The campground, once we stay, might be our next favorite part. ☺

Kanaskat-Palmer State Park

East of Black Diamond: Hiking, Biking, Wading, Fishing, Horseshoe Pits, Camping, Yurts

Season: Year-Round

Parking: Fair

Difficulty: 1/4

Time: Hrs to Days

Getting There: Input into GPS.

The Adventure: This park is best known for its Class Two through Class Four rapids. Please DO NOT attempt to float this river unless you have whitewater knowledge. This is a whitewater rafting trip, NOT a float. You can

seriously injure yourself and others if you attempt this without the proper knowledge and gear.

You can however enjoy the rolling rapids from afar. ☺ Our kids loved hearing the rushing water and seeing BIG rapids close up. They also loved clambering over the rocks and throwing rocks into the river. Fishing can be done from the shores for trout and salmon as well. There is plenty to do if you are not an expert whitewater rafter. ☺

The campground offers shade, nicely maintained campsites and partial hook up sites for RVs. Probably the most exciting option for sleeping in Kanaskat State Park are the six available yurts! Complete with a fire grill, picnic table, hookup for electricity, and an ADA accessible deck, you will be glamping in style. Add to that the proximity to the city and bathrooms with showers, it's no wonder this campground gets rave reviews online.

Our Favorite Part: The kids LOVED the raging river, huge boulders and rolling rapids! It's just so fun to see that stuff up close!

Snoqualmie Valley Trail

Season: Year-Round　　　**Difficulty:** 1/4

Parking: Variable　　　**Time:** 1-3 hrs

Getting There: Depends on where you want to start. For a list of parking areas go to this website. http://www.duvallwa.gov/DocumentCenter/View/500/Snoqualmie-Valley-Trail-Map?bidId=

The Adventure: At 31.5 miles the adventure is what you make it! The above website is really a great resource to refer to before your trip. The link brings you to a PDF from the City of Duvall which outlines the trail, parking, parks along the trail, salmon viewing locations, salmon safe farms along the trail and educational signage.

Our main use of this trail has been for short walks, runs, and bike rides. As our kids get older it would be fun to do a longer ride during the fall to check out the Salmon run and the changing leaves of the Valley.

Our Favorite Part: The untapped potential. Admittedly this is not one we've frequented.

Torguson Park

North Bend: Biking, Walking, Fields, Rock Wall,
Skate Park, BMX Bike Park, Playground

Season: Year-Round

Parking: Fair

Difficulty: 1-2/4

Time: 1.5 hrs

Getting There: It's easiest to put this into your GPS and follow the directions. Slow down as you get close because the turn is VERY easy to miss. You won't see the park until you turn in. If you're going for the BMX Bike Park you can put North Bend Les Schwab in your GPS. There is parking at the back of their lot, right next to the track.

The Adventure: Oh, sooooo many here!

At one end of the park they have one baseball field, a soccer field, a rock-climbing wall and a playground. In the middle they have four baseball diamonds. At the other end, they have a skate park and a BMX bike park! Connecting everything is over a mile of paved trail, great for bikes and or walking!

We by far spend the majority of our time at the bike park! Our kids started on the beginner track which is the small track to the right. In fact, our youngest used this track to learn how to start on his own without us holding the bike! Before we knew it, they were both riding the big tracks! A heads up, helmets are a must and there are experienced riders doing BIG things at this track. It is very family friendly though and the "Big Kids" are usually pretty good at watching out for the littles!

Our Favorite Part: The bike park!

Asahel Curtis Nature Trail

East of North Bend: Hiking, Nature Walks, Water

Season: Year-Round   **Difficulty:** 1-2/4

Parking: Variable   **Time:** 1.5 hrs

Getting There: There are two options for this trail. One option will be two miles round trip and the other one mile. To extend the hike, and get a more urban feel and easy parking, park at the Asahel Curtis Picnic Area. For an easier hike and a more natural feel, park at the Annette Lake/Asahel Curtis Parking Lot. Both lots require a National Forest day or annual pass.

Asahel Curtis Picnic Area: I-90 East Bound to exit 47. Take a left off the freeway. Go over the freeway and take a right at the stop sign after the bridge. Continue straight .3 miles into Asahel Curtis picnic area. As you're coming in you will see a dirt parking area that probably fits about six cars. The trailhead is just past that and is marked. There are additional parking spots as the road loops around and back to the main road.

Annette Lake/Asahel Curtis Parking: I-90 East Bound to exit 47. Turn right off the ramp and then left onto Forest Road 5590. Parking will be on your right in .3 miles.

The Adventure: Starting at the Asahel Curtis Picnic area definitely extends your adventure and gives you a bit more of a workout! Kids will love the old-fashioned water pump in the picnic area. You will love the fire pits and picnic benches, including one right on the water!

Starting the trail from this area creates a two-mile round-trip hike that goes through an area that will remind you of an urban hike complete with a graffiti bridge that you get to walk under and a man-made water run-off. The kids loved this little add on. We loved that it added distance and even had a short little climb. It meets up with the more well-known Asahel Curtis Nature Loop at the Annette Lake Trailhead. For an easier adventure you can start here. The trail is much more serene, well maintained and easy.

Our Favorite Part: We actually really loved the extension. The kids thought it was neat, and we loved the calmness and ease of parking. We didn't mind the less maintained part of the trail and the "urban" features. We would highly recommend it!

Tiger Mountain:

Swamp, Big Tree, Brink, Wetlands, Adventure and Bus Trail Loop

Season: Year-Round

Parking: Moderate

Difficulty: 1-2/4

Time: 1.5-2 hrs

Getting There: Take exit 20 off of I-90. Turn south (left turn if coming from Snoqualmie) off of freeway. Shortly thereafter turn right onto SE 79th St and continue up to the parking lot. A Discover Pass is required.

The Adventure: This loop is for the adventurous that don't mind following multiple turn directions! 😊 It sounds a little arduous, but it really is a fun loop! I got this idea from WTA, but please note that there is a wrong turn in there as of 2019! (oops) So please follow these directions!

Start out on the Swamp Trail. The kids will love reading the story of Zoe the swamp monster, and you'll love the canopy if it's a rainy day! This will end at the Puget Power Lines, where if you look around, you will find plentiful blackberries! Don't forget to look down for the smaller, sweeter, seedless trailing blackberry! **Continue onto the Big Tree Trail.** The Big Tree Trail meets the **Brink Trail, turn left.** The trail will cut across the Puget Power Trail where you will see a sign for the **Wetlands and Adventure Trail. Follow that** trail up a slight hill until you see a **three-way unmarked split in the path. You want to go on the trail to the FAR LEFT.** Follow the trail uphill until you come to **another unmarked split. This time you will have two options, go right.** You will come to a "T", go **right onto the Wetlands Trail.** The trail will take you by a small pond by the name of **Round Lake** and **onto the larger Puget Power trail.** When you get to the Puget Power Trail **go right.** Soon thereafter **on the left, you will see the Bus Trail.** Take that trail. This will take you by an

old, broken-down bus on its side that the kids will think is cool. **Back track just a bit to the Around the Lake Trail. Turn right** (it was on your left just before the bus). Soon thereafter, it will come to a two-way split, **stay right** to **continue onto the Around the Lake Trail** and follow it back to the parking lot.

This loop has a lot of turns including two unmarked turns. I bolded each step to make it easier to follow. Please be sure to take a map, or a map app with you to prevent getting lost! Total round trip on this fun adventure is approximately 3 miles.

Our Favorite Part: The variety of the story boards, HUGE tree, swamp, pond, tradition lake and an old broken-down bus!

Snoqualmie Falls

Season: Year-Round   **Difficulty:** 1-2/4

Parking: Variable   **Time:** .5-1.5 hrs

Getting There: I recommend parking in the lower lot. It is free, and you can hike up first which I find easier with beginners. You will pass the main lot and go about 1.5 miles toward Fall City. Slow down as you near the bottom of the hill, as the turn comes up fast! Turn left on 372nd. Turn left onto Fish Hatchery Road. Drive into the lower lot. Here is the address to the lower lot in case you want to enter it in your GPS.

37479 SE Fish Hatchery Road, Fall City 98024.

The Adventure: A great 1.5 mile round trip hike with AMAZING scenery! The short jaunt from the lower lot to the upper viewing deck is a great place to train legs for longer hikes as the pitch is good, but short. So just when you're thinking I don't want to keep going up…you're done! The trail is well maintained and full of beginner adventurers, so you won't feel like you're the only one huffing and puffing! A plus for small children is the gift shop at the top. I may have bribed my youngest with promises of an ice cream sandwich at some point. ☺ Kind of negates the hike but that day it was more for me and haha…I only took one bite! On the way down, we took the time to read all the educational posts regarding trees, vegetation, and electricity! Once at the bottom lot again, we followed the boardwalk to the lower viewing deck. A great mid-day adventure!

Our Favorite Part: The ease of the lower lot once you figure out how to get there! We love coming to the lower lot, walking to the end of the boardwalk, checking out the falls, and heading home. We do that far more than we hike the trail!

Cougar Mountain and Coal Creek Natural Area

Bellevue/Factoria: Hiking, Horseback Riding

Season: Year-Round   **Difficulty:** 1-4/4

Parking: Crowded   **Time:** 1-3 hrs

Getting There: Decide which trail(s) you would like to explore and get directions to the closest parking lot here.

https://www.kingcounty.gov/services/parks-recreation/parks/parks-and-natural-lands/popular-parks/cougar.aspx

The Adventure: When our kids were young this was our "Go-To" place to expose them to hiking. At the time, we lived in Renton. Its proximity, ease of use, and cool water features within less than a mile made it ideal for toddlers and parents who don't want to have the in or out (of the carrier) fight.

We always parked at the Red Town Trailhead and would cross the street to the Coal Creek Natural area outside of Cougar Mountain. Disclaimer: This is a VERY busy road. Please do not cross it if you're not comfortable. Jason and I would each pick up one kid, and we would run across as soon as it was clear. We felt comfortable with it. Admittedly though, that cross over needs a crosswalk.

Once you get to the other side you will see Coal Creek Trail. This is your trail 😊. Luckily, it's hard to miss! There is a very short downhill portion, and then the trail is flat. In about ¼ of a mile you will be at North Fork Falls, which was always a hit with the kids and a great photo opportunity! We started our kids on this trail at about age 2. It was perfect because they could make it the ¼ mile there and the ¼ mile back. We started pushing them further as they got more into it, and their endurance built up. After some time, they were ready for the bigger, easy loops in Cougar Mountain. As luck would have it, we moved to North Bend at that time, which brought us to great beginner trails within minutes verses the 20-25 minutes it used to take us to get to Cougar Mountain and

Coal Creek. To check out the larger network of trails that can be looped, go to the website listed under "Getting There." This website also has a trail map and mileage for

each section. Cougar Mountain really is a network of trails that can be connected to fit your needs for the day. You can opt for routes with more elevation gain or meandering paths. The choice is yours, and the versatility is a huge plus in our book!

Our Favorite Part:

The versatility to essentially create your own hike. If this were closer to us (we're in North Bend), we would likely be here much more often!

Deep Creek Trail

Snoqualmie Ridge: Hiking, Biking, Playground, Water, Field Play

Season: Year-Round   **Difficulty:** 2/4

Parking: Plentiful   **Time:** 1-2 hours

Getting There: Input Azalea Park into your GPS/phone. Park. The trail is marked with a sign at the back end of the playground and field.

The Adventure: The trail starts off going downhill. We weren't sure how the kids would do coming back up, but luckily the downhill trek is short lived and so is the up! This is a nice all-around trail with not too much elevation gain. I'm sure in the fall this trail is beautiful with fall foliage. We went in the summer. It was easily accessible, had full service restrooms and a playground! On the hike there were lots of berries, rocks, sticks, a stream and a bridge to explore! We even found some black raspberries, a rare treat! The hike can easily be extended by taking it the .84 miles up to the Snoqualmie Valley Trail. Once on the Snoqualmie Valley Trail, your adventures are endless, as this trail is 29 miles and connects to the larger Iron Horse Trail.

Our Favorite Part: The bridge, the water, restrooms, easy parking and a playground.

Tinkham Campground

Season: May-Sept   **Difficulty:** 2/4

Parking: Included   **Time:** Min. 1 day

Getting There: Take I-90 East to exit 42. Exit and take a right off the ramp. Go across the river. Follow the road as it bends to the left. The campground is in approximately 1 mile on your left hand side.

The Adventure: It is true that Tinkham has some road noise being so close to the freeway. None the less, we love this campground. With the river right there, you can just imagine the road is the river. It's all white noise, right? It's a great spot for walk-ins with 18 available. It's not too busy with through traffic, making it fun and comfortable for the kids to ride their bikes around the campsite and the parents to relax! There was river access (small) at one point as well as a great hiking trail extending off the main campground loop. The kids had a blast riding their bikes on this trail and getting their first "real mountain bike" experience! At the end of the trail we found a beautiful pond with its own viewing "deck".   Being so close to the Valley with great walk-in availability makes this an excellent first time Campground for the more adventurous! Why the more adventurous? Well, it's built with good ol' fashioned vault toilets…a fancy name for outhouses. Some of our other choices have "real" bathrooms and even showers. For some people these are camping musts, but if they're not, Tinkham could be a great fit!

What we loved: Tinkham has some "special" sites down by the water. They are larger and more spread out. We were able to get one of these and loved inviting friends from North Bend in for a campfire and 'smores! The kids loved playing with friends and riding their bikes. Great all-around experience!

Denny Creek Hike

East of North Bend: Hiking, Natural Water Slides and Pools, Nearby Camping

Season: May-Oct   **Difficulty:** 2/4

Parking: Crowded   **Time:** 2-4 hours

Getting There: Take I-90 East to Exit 47. Turn left off the freeway. Go over the freeway and make a right at the stop sign after the bridge. Go .2 miles and turn left toward Denny Creek, Denny Creek Campground and Franklin Falls. At 1.7 miles you will cross a bridge. Keep going. At 2 miles you will see the campground on the left. Keep going. At 2.2 miles you will see a sign that says 58. Not sure what they mean by this but turn left at that marker. Almost immediately you will cross over a bridge. In .2 miles you will come to the parking lot. You will need a NWF pass, annual or daily $5.

The Adventure: This is a warm summer's day adventure for sure! The trick is to time it to climb it in the morning, stay for lunch and a swim as the weather warms up and hike down in the heat 😊. It's a much better option in my eyes than hiking up in the heat. The kids will likely be wet from swimming. So, they're not bothered at all, and when the kids are happy the parents are happy! The adventure can really last all day if you want it to! Be sure to bring swim clothes, towels, sunscreen and proper hiking shoes. It's just a way more pleasant hike up if everyone's wearing proper gear! The trail is a beautiful, well shaded, great beginner trail and with a summer wonderland natural water park for the kids, why not!? At approximately 2.5 miles roundtrip, it's perfect!

Note: You can extend this hike to Keekwulee Falls making the trip approximately 5 miles…although our kids have not made it past the water!

Our Favorite Part: The water!!!

Franklin Falls

East of North Bend: Hiking, Waterfall and Natural Water Pools

Season: May-Oct   **Difficulty:** 2/4

Parking: Crowded   **Time:** 1.5-2.5 hrs

Getting There: Take I-90 East to Exit 47. Turn left off the freeway. Go over the freeway and make a right at the stop sign after the bridge. Go .2 miles and turn left toward Denny Creek, Denny Creek Campground and Franklin Falls. At 1.7 miles you will cross a bridge. Keep going. At 2 miles you will see the campground on the left. Keep going. At 2.2 miles you will see a sign that says 58.

Continue PAST the marker. Just after marker 58 you will
see a newer large parking lot on the right. Park near the
end of the lot. At the end of the lot you will find the
connector trail that goes down to marker 58. The trailhead
for Franklin Falls is across from marker 58 before the
bridge on the right. (Toward Denny Creek). You will need
a NWF pass, annual or daily $5.

The Adventure: Spectacular views of an amazing
waterfall at the end preceded by views of the river along a
beautiful and well-kept trail. This trail is short which
makes it perfect for kids and beginners. One thing to note
though are some safety points. There are multiple places
along the trail that have view points where you can look
down at the river. Although it's been awhile since doing
this hike, I distinctly remember wanting the kids in our
group to stay with us verses running ahead due to these
drop off view-points. I was so worried that one of them
was going to slip right off the edge and tumble down to the
river! Granted, I'm a slightly paranoid parent, but

noteworthy none the less! Lastly, the final approach to the falls is narrow and rocky. I personally didn't feel very comfortable with our youngest in the pack on my husband's back as we scrambled that final approach. Luckily, he's sure footed, and everyone made it just fine.

Our Favorite Part: The massive waterfall at the end and the "wading" pools. The kids loved taking their shoes and socks off and getting their feet wet!

NWF Tree Cutting Adventure

East of North Bend: Maps and Permits at the North Bend Ranger Station

Season: Nov-Dec   **Difficulty:** 2/4

Parking: NA   **Time:** 1.5-2.5 hrs

Getting There: There are many places to go. The North Bend Ranger Station has a map for areas before Snoqualmie pass. We usually go east of Snoqualmie Pass to the Wenatchee National Forest, as we meet up with friends from the East Side. If you do choose to go east of Snoqualmie Pass you will need to check in with their local ranger station, as it's a different permit and a different map!

The Adventure: Cutting down your very own Christmas Tree!!! Check in at the North Bend Ranger Station for your $10 permit (at the time of this writing) and a map. You'll need a high clearance all wheel drive vehicle, a hand saw or chainsaw and warm clothes! We've done this as an annual event with friends usually on the Friday after Thanksgiving. We head up to the snow line, find an area off the forest service road where we can park several cars and we tailgate with snacks and hot cocoa while the kids play in the snow! After some snow play and snacks we adventure out on the roads and into the woods a bit looking for that perfect tree. Our favorite spots: Hansen Creek (exit 47), Stampede Pass (exit 62) and Amabilis Mountain (exit 63). If you go East of the Summit you will need a Wenatchee National Forest Tree Permit. They can be bought at Pioneer Coffee in Cle Elum.

Safety Note: If you are going to drive up into the snow be careful. Know the road conditions and make sure you are prepared with chains for your all-wheel drive (yes, all-wheel drive). Road conditions can be confirmed with your local ranger station. A shovel, traction pads and a tow strap are also good to have. Additionally, we recommend that you travel with friends. Above all else, do not drive into conditions that you are not comfortable with. You can always park your car and walk.

Our Favorite Part: In the words of our son, "All of It!"

Snoqualmie River Float

Snoqualmie to Fall City: Tubes, Rafts, Kayaks

Season: June-September   **Difficulty:** 2/4

Parking: Crowded   **Time:** 4 hrs

Plum Boat Launch Two

Getting There: You will put in at Plum Boat Launch #2. There is a #1, but it has some more advanced rapids. Beginners are best advised to put in at #2, below the rapids. To get there from Snoqualmie you will drive past the Salish Lodge and the Falls viewing entrance. Start your descent toward Fall City. At the bottom of the hill, you will turn left onto 372nd toward SE Fish Hatchery Road. It is your first left hand turn at the bottom of the hill. Follow 372nd until it intersects with SE Fish Hatchery Road. Turn right and take it to the second pull out. Your first pull out will be on your left-hand side, just as you turn onto SE Fish Hatchery Road. The second one is shortly after, also on the left-hand side. Each will have a sign encouraging water safety and showing you the route.

If you miss 372nd you can take 361st to SE Fish Hatchery Road. Turn left instead of right and Plum Boat Launch #2 will be your first boat launch turn out.

The Adventure: Some use Plum Boat Launch #2 for swimming and wading purposes only given its beautiful sandy beach. It also serves as a great put in point for floating the Snoqualmie River. Our youngest has not done this yet. Jason did the float with our oldest (7 at the time) and some friends. They all loved it. The float is an easy float with occasional class one rapids. At the end of the season when water is low the river can get slow and may require occasional walking. Plan on four hours total to get to the Fall City take out points. You can take out on either side of the river at Raging River or Fall City Community Parks.

Given the length and the occasional class one rapids we don't recommend doing this with kids younger than 6 unless you have experience with rafting and trust your expertise.

Fall City Community Park Take Out

Frequently people will bring an extra smaller tube with a bottom in it and put food and beverages in that and then tie it to their group. When Jason and his friend took our oldest and three additional kids, all the tubes were tied together. Their extra storage tube was tied to them. Sunscreen and sunglasses are a good idea as well as waterproof bags for anything that can't get wet! Lastly, always wear life vests and enjoy the float!

Our Favorite Part: This was the only adventure I didn't do but our kiddo's favorite part was the rapids!

Middle Fork Campground

Northeast of North Bend: Hiking, Nature Walks, Water, Biking, Fishing, Camping

Season: May-September   **Difficulty:** 2/4

Parking: Included   **Time:** Days

Getting There: Take exit 34 off of I-90 in North Bend. Turn left onto 468th. Turn right on SE Middle Fork road in about ½ a mile. The road will fork. Lake Dorothy road is the upper fork. Stay on the lower road which is the continuation of the Middle Fork Road. You will be on this road for approximately another 10 miles. This is one I would enter into the GPS, as Middle Fork Road takes some unclear "turns" or deviations early on before it becomes a

Predictable, newly paved wide road. At the end of this nice newly paved road is a left-hand turn into the campground.

The Adventure: We love this close to home adventure! It's one of the more spread out campgrounds in the area giving you a sense of privacy which we love. It also features four double sites that work well for small groups of 12 or less (sites 1, 2, 4, and 7). Next to these campsites are two group sites that will fit 25 or less (site 3 and site 6). These spots are ideal for family friends to adventure out together! The campsites offer a variety of shade levels at different times of the day. It's always great to bring a pop-up canopy tent to offer shade on a hot day! Less than a mile from these double and group sites is the river which offers some fun swimming/wading holes to cool off in that hot summer sun. There are also numerous hiking trails nearby and even leaving the campground. At 39 sites, the campground has minimal traffic once full for the weekend, making it a great place to ride bikes as well!

Toilets are vault and you won't find running water, playgrounds, basketball courts or other amenities making this a level 2/4 for the extra "roughing it" factor. 😊

Our Favorite Part: How close this quiet get-away is! The summer of 2017 was amazing as all sites were walk-in! Unfortunately, it is back to reservation, and only 7 sites are walk in now. 😣

Twin Falls: Ollalie State Park

North Bend: Hiking, Nature Walks, Water, Photography

Season: Year-Round   **Difficulty:** 2/4

Parking: Crowded   **Time:** 1.5-3 hrs

Getting There: Take exit 34 off I-90. Turn right onto 468ᵗʰ. Before the bridge turn left onto 160ᵗʰ. You will see a small Ollalie State Park sign on the right of the road indicating the left turn. Follow 160ᵗʰ to the end. You will need a day or annual Discover Pass

The Adventure: This is an explorer's adventure for sure! Our kids' favorite hike, this is adjustable for length and difficulty, easy to access, and full of river shores, creeks, rocks, trees, and even a large waterfall to explore!

We started this adventure with our kids by first walking
along the start of the trail and along the river. Then we
made it a goal to get to the first view point, a bench, which
is one mile up. Several times we hiked to this bench where
we ate lunch and checked out the falls; then we turned
back. Once our kids were easily hiking up to the bench, we
decided to go all the way. It's important that you are
feeling great at the bench, because going the full distance
doubles your hike from 2 to 4
miles round trip. It's not a
hard hike, but it doubles the
distance so make sure
everyone's ready. Once
ready, the extra length is well
worth the time and energy!
The trail takes you over the
falls onto a bridge! After the
bridge, there is one more look
out about ¼ of a mile (if that)
up the trail. If you keep
going, the trail will meet up

with the Iron Horse Trail. We normally turn around at the bridge.

On your way back, (or on the way up), there is a long staircase that leads down to a lookout just below the bridge. The trail consists of several steps, but if your knees can take it, do it! It's a wonderful frontal view of the falls.

Tip: Stop at the bench for a quick snack, the bridge for another quick snack, and lunch at the bench ON THE WAY BACK DOWN. This will sustain your energy levels through the hike.

Our Favorite Part: The ability to adapt this trail to fit our needs for the day!

Duthie Hill Mountain Bike Park

Season: Year-Round   **Difficulty:** 2-4+/4

Parking: Crowded   **Time:** 1-3 hrs

Getting There: Take I-90 Westbound to exit 18 Issaquah Highlands. Turn right onto Highlands drive. Stay on it for approximately 2 miles. Turn right onto Issaquah Fall City Road. Go about 2 miles. Turn right at Endeavor Elementary School onto Issaquah Fall City Road. You read that right, turn right onto Issaquah Fall City Road, **from** Issaquah Fall City Road. I know but do it anyway. The parking lot will be on your left. The parking lot holds 74 vehicles, but it gets VERY busy. Some people park on the road, others park at Endeavor Elementary School (during non-school hours).

The Adventure: Oh, there are SO many adventures here, and we honestly haven't explored them all. Trail difficulty is rated on the same system as skiing. Green circles are the easiest, followed by blue squares, black diamonds and double black diamonds. If you're looking for flowy fun adventure look no further than the green circles or possibly (work your way up to) the blue squares. Keep in mind that Duthie Hill is a bike park. There are numerous stunts found outside of the green terrain, and even some easy "stunts" found on the green terrain.

Important to note is that everyone is required to ride the Connector Trail from the parking lot to the actual bike park. My first time here, I found this confusing. The Connector Trail is a green trail that connects to the main Access Road that goes into the central clearing area AKA basecamp. You will find a map there, restrooms, a covered picnic area, and a small BMX-like bike park and log rides. You are not able to drive to this area.

Once you turn left onto the Access Road from the Connector, you will start an easy climb which peaks quickly and then descends into the base area. Near the top of that peak, you will see a sign for Bootcamp on the right. A small, (couple hundred feet), trail will go from the Access Road to Bootcamp, where it will appear that you can go right or left. All trails are one-way at Duthie. Go left, it will take you to the base area.

We took this fun single track into the base area verses staying on the wide access road. Staying on the access road will take you into the base area, but it's not as much fun! If you are riding with young kids, or there are people in your group just starting their journey, I would turn around at base camp after doing the downhill portion of Bootcamp.

For the quick and easy version take the access road back. For a lengthier version take Bootcamp back to your original access point. Bootcamp is a loop and it's one direction, so you will start at the end opposite to where you rode in. Referencing the map should help you find Bootcamp's start point. Once back at your original entrance point on Bootcamp off the access road, jump back onto the access road, and then back to your car.

It was kind of a bummer for my seven-year-old and I turning around right when we got there, but for my four-year-old it was PLENTY. My four-year-old was riding a BMX bike. Total riding time from the Connector, to the Access Road, to Bootcamp (left turn) to the base area BMX park and then back to the car on the access road was probably 1¼ hours and PLENTY for him. Unless your four-year-old is a seasoned rider, I don't recommend them hitting up Duthie. Irregardless of age, the child or individual needs to be an experienced rider on flat dirt trails, turns, small ups and downs, and pavement.

My seven-year-old on the other hand was begging for more! So, her and I went back another time! We hit The Connector, The Access Trail, all of Bootcamp, the Luna Lines, and the bike park. We would have stayed longer, but unfortunately, we were on a time line. This was by far the most fun I had riding with our kids this summer and I can't wait to go back next year when BOTH our kids are riding gear bikes!

Safety Note: Helmets and water are a must. Riding gloves and snacks are great ideas. If you are riding with kids, it is always a good idea to try the trail first before taking your kids on it. Also, if you are new, it is a great idea to go with a friend who is familiar with the park or sign up for an introductory class through Evergreen Mountain Bike Alliance, Sweet Lines, or similar programs.

Our Favorite Part: The fun set up of the park. It's really set up like a little mini ski resort with its central base area with trails heading up from there and back down. Ratings were familiar to our kids with green circles, blue squares and so on, and the variety was a blast! Highly recommend this adventure!

Lodge Lake

Summit West at Snoqualmie: Hiking

Season: Late June-Oct   **Difficulty:** 3/4

Parking: Plentiful   **Time:** 2.5-3.5 hrs

Getting There: Take I-90 East to Exit 52. Turn right toward Summit West Ski Area. Turn into the parking lot at Summit West (almost immediately after the freeway). You will be able to turn left to short term parking or right to the general parking lot. The general parking lot will fork into three directions. The lower lot is immediately to your right next to the main road. Then there is a middle lot and an upper lot. Drive to the end of the middle lot. You will see a PCT sign at the entrance. This is the trail you will take to get to Lodge Lake.

The Adventure: This is a great more aggressive beginner hike on the Pacific Crest Trail. At approximately 4 miles round trip with over 800-foot elevation gain it's a great step up for kids and adults that are ready to progress with their hiking! You will start out on the Pacific Crest Trail, heading left through the trees towards the open ski hill. The first part of this hike will take you up the hill under the Pacific Crest Chair lift. The trail then heads over the crest, into the forest and down the back side of the mountain. Heading toward the lake, the trail has some steeper steps. Once we got to the lake it was beautiful, calm, and a bit marshy. Our kids LOVED hiking the ski hill and getting to see the back side of a hill that they ski in the winter! Although we haven't, you can continue on the Pacific Crest Trail (the Pacific Crest Trail runs from the Northern border of Washington down to the California and Mexico border).

Our Favorite Part: The nostalgia of hiking our local ski hill!

Cedar Butte

Season: Year-Round

Parking: Plentiful

Difficulty: 3/4

Time: 2-2.5 hrs

Getting There: Take Exit 32 in North Bend and turn South (right turn if coming from Snoqualmie). Head up Cedar Falls Road to Rattlesnake Lake. Follow road to the left rather than turning into Rattlesnake Lake. Immediately there will be a left-hand turn into state park parking. Since it's a State Park, you will need a $10 day pass or $30 annual pass. You can park at the lake for free, but parking

can get VERY difficult on warm days. Park and head to the Iron Horse Trail.

The Adventure: This is a great hike for kids that have already mastered up to the bench at Twin Falls but may or may not have done the whole trip. This hike is just under 4 miles round trip with the first and last mile being flat on the Iron Horse Trail. You will start off from the parking lot to the Iron Horse Trail. At approximately one mile in, there will be a trail on the right with a very small Cedar Butte sign on a tree. Start looking for the trail after the bridge; this will ensure that you don't miss your turn! Head up the trail. Roughly ½ a mile up, the trail will fork. The trail to the right is about ½ mile longer than the trail to the left, but the trail to the left is steeper. I normally go to the right on the way up and stay right on the way down, which allows me to do the more challenging section on the downhill. ☺ At the top, you will have a great view and a nice spot to sit and eat lunch or snacks. Our youngest did this at four which is probably a good minimum age for this hike, unless your kid is a seasoned hiker.

Our Favorite Part: The view, and the great, short training grounds for longer hikes

A Thank You

A huge thank you goes out to my family. My husband and kids were my partners in exploration as we hit the road looking for adventure nearly every weekend! Looking back on our summer of exploration makes me yearn for next summer and for me that's saying a lot! Although I love my summers, I am always excited to see the winter! With that first snowfall we are typically up at the hill playing in the snow or even putting on skis! That said, the journey of writing this book has made me appreciate summers and even our shoulder seasons that much more. There are so many adventures out there to be had. You don't have to be a professional. A little knowledge on what to bring and where to go will take you a long way. I hope you enjoy this book, and that it becomes a catalyst for getting you, and your family outside!

About the Author

As a native of Washington State, the love of the outdoors instilled itself at a very early age. In her younger years Tiffany enjoyed biking, hiking and skiing. While at Western Washington University, from 1998-2002, she *really* fell in love with all the outdoors had to offer. From hiking, to biking, to skiing, camping, backpacking, sailing and rock climbing. She was fortunate to have opportunities to try a variety of the local adventures. Skiing, hiking, camping, and biking have stayed with her through the years. She met her husband at Chiropractic College in 2003 in Hayward California. A Washington native himself, the two married in 2008, moved back to Washington in 2009, and started Snoqualmie Optimal Health Chiropractic in 2012. In 2016, the family moved from Renton to North Bend. Dr. Tiffany and Dr. Jason have two kids, born in 2011 and 2013.

Resources

https://www.outdoorproject.com/

https://www.wta.org/

https://parks.state.wa.us/

https://www.fs.fed.us/

https://www.recreation.gov/

https://www.alltrails.com/

https://www.evergreenmtb.org/

Washington State Parks: A Complete Recreation Guide by Marge and Ted Mueller

Best Hikes with Kids: Western Washington and the Cascades by Joan Burton and Ira Spring

Index

Chronicle *Your* Adventures

Please use these blank pages to write your own adventures!

Chronicle *Your* Dreams

Made in the USA
Columbia, SC
25 March 2019